SEASONS SEASONS SEASONS SEASONS

SPRING

Moira Butterfield

Illustrated by Helen James

A⁺

Smart Apple Media

Published by Smart Apple Media
2140 Howard Drive West, North Mankato, MN 56003

Designed and illustrated by Helen James
Tree illustration page 24 Moira Butterfield

Photographs by Corbis (Mark E. Gibson, Lindsay Hebberd, Steve Kaufman,
Matthias Kulka, Danny Lehman, Joe McDonald, Roy Morsch, Roger Ressmeyer,
Christian Sarramon, Craig Tuttle)

Printed and bound in Thailand

Library of Congress Cataloging-in-Publication Data

Butterfield, Moira.
Spring / by Moira Butterfield.
p. cm. — (Seasons)
Includes index.
ISBN 1-58340-614-X
1. Spring—Juvenile literature. I. Title.

QB637.5.B88 2005
508.2—dc22   2005042577

First Edition

9 8 7 6 5 4 3 2 1

Contents

All about spring

Spring is a season, a busy, lively time when animal babies are born and flowers begin to blossom.

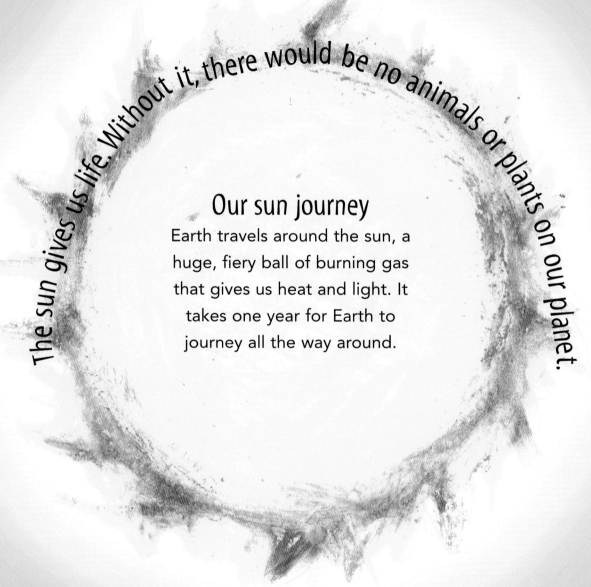

The sun gives us life. Without it, there would be no animals or plants on our planet.

Our sun journey

Earth travels around the sun, a huge, fiery ball of burning gas that gives us heat and light. It takes one year for Earth to journey all the way around.

Earth words

The two halves of Earth are called the northern and southern hemispheres. While one has spring, the other has fall. The area around the middle of Earth is called the equator.

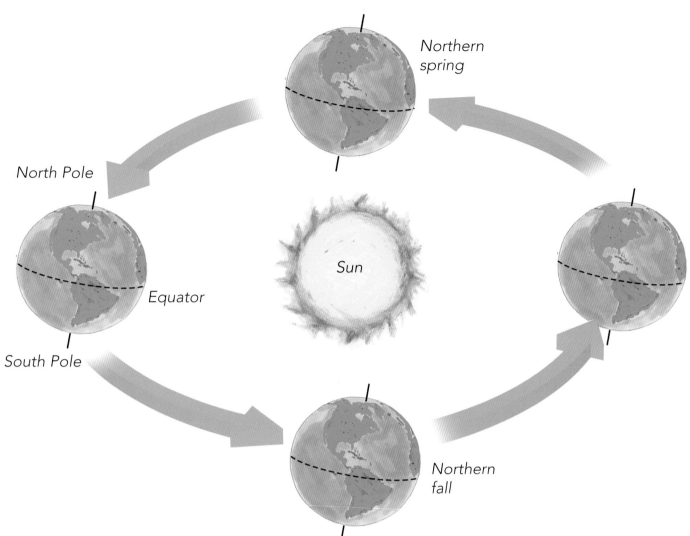

North Pole

Equator

South Pole

Northern
spring

Sun

Northern
fall

Here comes spring

As Earth travels around the sun, the seasons change. First one half and then the other half of the planet begins to tilt toward the sun. Spring arrives for you when your half of Earth begins to face the sun and comes closer to its warming rays.

Time for changes

Spring is an exciting season because it brings lots of change. The weather gradually grows warmer and warmer until spring finally turns into summer.

5

My spring, your spring

Spring comes at different times around the world. Trees near you might have spring flowers, while trees on the other side of the world are losing their leaves.

Spring north
In Earth's northern half, spring comes in March, April, and May.

Spring south
In Earth's southern half, spring comes in September, October, and November.

What about the middle?
In countries along the equator, it is hot year-round. There is no separate spring or fall. Places near the equator have wet and dry seasons instead.

Days and nights

As Earth travels around the sun, it spins in space like a top. It takes 24 hours to spin once. First one side faces the sun, then the other, giving us days and nights. In the spring, the days grow longer and the nights get shorter.

The big melt

In the far north and south of the world, the sea is frozen in the winter. Then, when spring comes, the ice begins to melt. It breaks into floating chunks called icebergs. They can be as big as buildings.

Ships must watch out for icebergs during the spring.

Light comes back

The North and South Poles are in darkness for six months of the year, during fall and winter. When spring arrives, they are bathed in daylight again, and it stays light for six whole months.

Spring's coming

When spring arrives, the world of animals and plants seems to wake up after a long winter sleep. Here are some spring signs to look for.

Listen to spring

Birds start to sing a lot in the spring. They are sending messages to other birds like them. They might be trying to attract a mate or to tell other birds to keep away from their home.

Smell spring

Lots of trees flower in the spring, and the blossoms often have a strong perfume. The smell attracts insects that come and feed on the nectar stored inside the flowers.

Trees blossom and birds sing in spring.

Spring gets busy

Spring gradually grows warmer and warmer as the months go by. More and more animals come out. Plants start to grow new leaves and flowers. For nature, it is the busiest season of the year!

Busy crawling

When it's warm enough, insects hatch and start to crawl around. Worms come up to the surface of the ground, too. They have been hiding deep down in the soil during the winter.

Busy swimming

Ponds become much more lively places. You might see insects skimming the surface, and gnats flying overhead. Frogs lay their eggs in tiny balls of jelly called spawn.

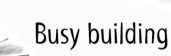

Busy building

You might see birds collecting twigs and pieces of grass. They are building their nests and getting ready to lay eggs.

Spring weather

In the spring, the weather grows warmer, but it might not be sunny. There could be rain showers and puddles to splash in. You might even see a rainbow.

Why does it rain?

1. The sun heats up the water on Earth. Some of the water evaporates, which means it turns into a very fine mist called vapor.

2. The vapor rises into the air. As it goes higher in the sky, it gets cooler. This makes it change back into water droplets.

3. The water droplets gather together to make clouds in the sky. The droplets gradually grow bigger and bigger.

4. Eventually, the droplets are so big and heavy that they fall back to Earth as rain.

Clouds are different shapes and colors. The darkest ones carry the most rain.

Clouds move across the sky because the wind blows them.

Rainbow season

Rainbows appear when the sun comes out on a rainy day. It shines on raindrops in the air. To see one, the sun must be behind you.

Sunlight usually looks clear to us, but it is actually made up of seven different colors. Raindrops split the light into the seven colors, which appear in the sky as a rainbow.

Rainbows always have the same seven colors: red, orange, yellow, green, blue, indigo, and violet.

Spring garden

In the spring, sunshine and rain help plants begin growing and flowering.

Why flowers have petals

Inside a flower are tiny parts for making fruit and seeds. There are also grains of pollen and a supply of sweet nectar. The flower petals protect these parts.

Passing pollen around

A flower needs pollen from another flower before it can grow fruit and seeds. Insects carry pollen between flowers when they feed on nectar.

Why flowers are different

Some flowers are bright and scented to attract insects. Other flowers rely on the wind to blow away their pollen. They are often small and pale.

Tulips grow from bulbs. In the spring, thousands of them flower in the fields of Holland.

All about bulbs

Some spring plants grow from bulbs hidden underground. Inside a bulb is a bud, some tiny leaves, and a store of food for the plant.

Time to flower

When the weather gets warmer, the bulb starts to sprout. It uses the food store to grow taller. Its flower grows bigger and starts to bloom in the sunshine.

Spring farm

Spring is a busy season on the farm. There are crops to plant and new animals to look after.

Planting season

In the winter, the ground is frozen hard, but it starts to thaw when spring comes. This is a good time for farmers to plant crops that will grow in the spring sunshine and rain.

Sowing the seeds

Farmers can plant lots of seeds in the ground using a machine called a seed drill. On small farms in some parts of the world, farmers scatter the seeds by hand instead.

A farmer uses a seed drill to sow cotton seeds in California.

Come outside!

Farm animals such as cows are often kept inside barns during the winter. When spring comes and the grass starts to grow, they are taken to the fields again.

Grass—yum, yum!

Animals that eat plants such as grass are called herbivores. Cows, sheep, and goats are all herbivores. They chew the grass and use it to make milk.

Happy birthday, lambs

Lambs are often born in the spring. This is a good time to be born because there is lots of grass for the ewes (mother sheep) to eat. This helps them make milk for their babies.

Spring animals

Some animals journey to new places, build homes, and give birth to new babies in the spring.

On the move

As the weather changes, lots of animals migrate. They travel from their winter home to a new home where they can find food and warmth in the spring and summer.

Look up

In the spring, some birds fly thousands of miles from their winter homes to their summer ones. Watch for flocks crossing the skies. They are a signal that spring is here!

Amazing monarchs

Some insects migrate in the spring. Millions of monarch butterflies make an amazing journey from Mexico to the Great Lakes. On the way, they lay eggs and die. When the eggs hatch, the new butterflies finish the journey.

Stay away!

Birds build their nests to try to keep egg-eating enemies away. They make it hard for enemy raiders by building nests high in trees, on steep cliffs, or in hidden burrows.

A huge flock of seabirds gathers in a bay in Alaska.

Springtime crowds

In the spring, seabirds often gather in huge groups called colonies to build nests and lay eggs. Thousands of birds arrive at the same nesting sites every year.

Spring babies

Many animal babies are born in the spring, when it is warm and there is lots of food to eat.

All kinds of eggs

Birds lay eggs in the spring. Wild bird eggs are often speckled so they blend into the background. This makes it harder for egg-eating enemies to spot them.

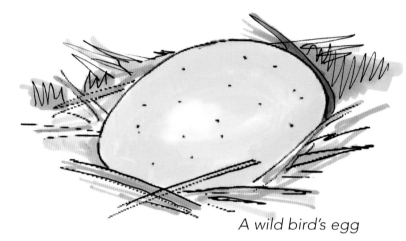

A wild bird's egg

A frog's eggs, called frogspawn.

Sea babies

In the spring, lots of sea animals spawn, which means they lay tiny eggs. Some crabs crawl from the sea to the beach and lay hundreds of eggs that wash into the sea and hatch.

River babies

Fish eggs hatch in rivers and lakes. The tiny babies are called fry. Frogspawn also hatch into tadpoles. Lots of the tadpoles and fish fry are eaten by other creatures, but some survive and grow into adults.

A tadpole hatches from an egg and slowly grows into a frog.

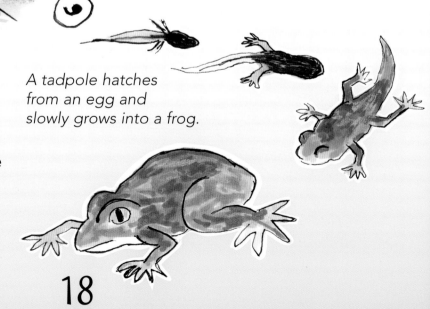

Ice babies

Imagine being born on a chunk of floating ice! That's what happens to baby seals in the far north in the spring. The mother seals give birth on ice chunks to try to protect their babies from hungry polar bears.

Hungry babies

Female polar bears give birth to baby twins in the winter, in a cozy den hidden under the snow. The babies come out for the first time in the spring. They follow their mother around as she hunts for food.

Polar bear babies come out for the first time in the spring.

Spring stories

All over the world, there are legends about springtime. Here are two.

The myth of Persephone

The Ancient Greeks told many stories about their gods and goddesses. We call these stories myths. This one explains why winter ends and spring begins.

The Ancient Greek goddess of Earth's plants was called Demeter. She tended the world's crops and made them grow, helped by her daughter Persephone.

One day, Persephone was kidnapped by Pluto, the god of the underworld. He took her back to the underworld to make her his wife.

Demeter was heartbroken to lose her daughter, and she stopped caring for the world's plants while she went searching for her. When Demeter found where Persephone had gone, she complained to Zeus (the king of the gods) and refused to let any plants grow on Earth.

Eventually, Zeus came up with a way around the problem. For three months of the year, Persephone had to stay with her husband in the underworld. The rest of the time, she could visit her mother on Earth. When Persephone is away, it is winter and plants stop growing. When she returns, spring begins, and everything starts to bloom again.

The rainbow and the pot of gold

In Irish legend, spring is thought to be a time when fairies are powerful. One type of Irish fairy is called a leprechaun, and legend has it that if you find one, he must grant you a wish.

Leprechauns are mischievous, and they have a secret stash of gold. People say that they hide it in a pot at the end of a rainbow. Here is the story.

There was once a greedy old couple living in Ireland. One day, the old woman found a leprechaun in her vegetable garden.

"You can have one wish. I'll be back tomorrow to grant it," he said, and then he disappeared.

When he came back the next day, the old couple demanded riches, fine clothes, a grand house, and all sorts of other luxuries.

"Stop! You are being selfish!" the leprechaun shouted. "I won't grant you anything!"

"But you must! We are poor!" the couple complained.

"All right, I'll give you a clue. I have hidden a pot of gold at the end of a rainbow. If you can find it, you'll be rich," the leprechaun replied, winked, and disappeared.

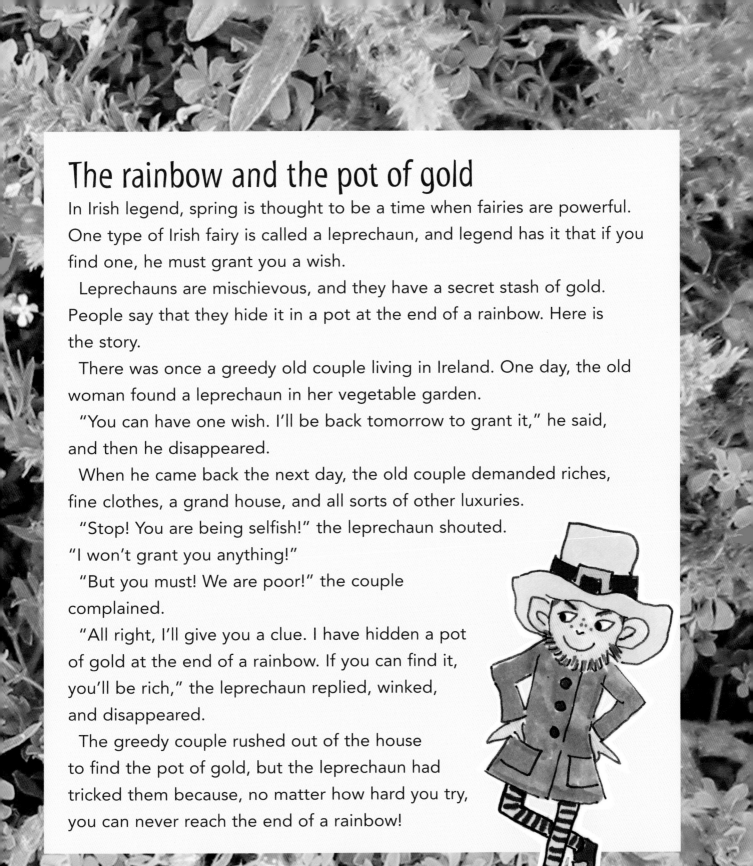

The greedy couple rushed out of the house to find the pot of gold, but the leprechaun had tricked them because, no matter how hard you try, you can never reach the end of a rainbow!

Spring parties

The start of spring is called the equinox. It falls on March 21st in the northern hemisphere. In the south, it is September 21st. People celebrate with parties.

Hindu Holi

In the spring, Hindu people celebrate Holi to thank their gods for the harvest to come. Sometimes it's called the festival of colors because people have fun splashing colored water everywhere and painting themselves with bright paint. There are big processions and bonfires. People throw coconuts and wheat into the fire for their gods and goddesses.

Spring stars

The Pleiades stars arrive in the northern sky in the spring, and Native American tribes hold feasts. Cherokee Indian legend says that the seven stars are seven boys who changed into stars when their mother punished them for being naughty.

Bun bang fai

In northern Thailand, in a place called Amphor Muang, people celebrate Bun Bang Fai in the spring. Bun Bang Fai means "rocket festival." Local people launch giant, home-made bamboo rockets, hoping to shake up the sky so the monsoon rains will start and help their rice grow.

Spring snake

The northern spring equinox is special at Chichén Itzá in Mexico. The afternoon sun casts a moving shadow on the wall of the old Mayan pyramid of El Castillo. The temple is built so the shadow-shape of the Mayan snake-god Kukulcán seems to slither down the side of the pyramid to a sacred spot at the bottom.

Paint the spring

Here are some ideas for making spring pictures.

Make your picture pastel

In the spring, lots of flowers blossom in soft pastel colors. You can make pastel shades by mixing colors with white. Pale pink, pale blue, and pale yellow are all pastels.

Blossom picture

In Japan, the spring cherry blossom is famous for its beauty. Paint a flowering tree on dark paper so that the flowers stand out. First, paint a trunk and some branches. Then add blobs of pale pink for the blossoms.

Spring field

Here are some tips for painting a field of spring flowers.

1. Paint two-thirds of your paper pale green. Let it dry, then paint the sky along the top pale blue.

2. When the sky is dry, paint two hedges, one along the back of the field and one closer to the front. This will make the field look 3D.

3. Use red, white, blue, and yellow dots of different sizes to make flowers in the field. The flower dots closest to the front should be bigger than the flowers at the back.

4. Put some tiny sheep at the back of the field, behind the first hedgerow. They will help to give your picture depth.

Make a piece of spring

Make an Easter egg basket or a spring flower.

Easter egg basket

Eggs are symbols of Easter, the Christian spring festival. Make a pretty basket and put some chocolate eggs inside for an Easter gift. You will need tracing paper, stiff colored paper, a ruler, pencil, scissors, and glue or tape.

1. Trace the basket template on this page. Transfer the shape to the colored paper and cut it out.

2. Fold along the dotted lines and glue or tape the basket together. Decorate it any way you like.

3. Cut a strip of paper and glue it to the inside of the basket to make a handle.

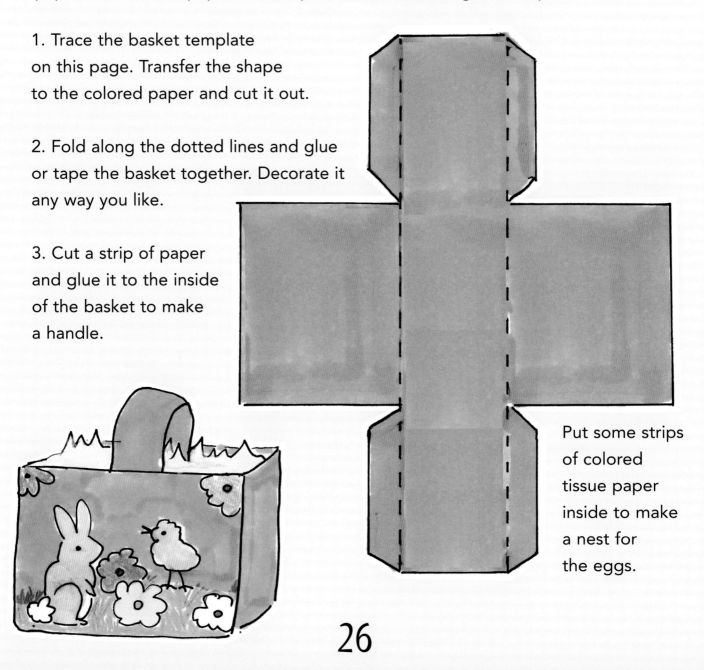

Put some strips of colored tissue paper inside to make a nest for the eggs.

Spring flower

Make a bunch of pretty spring flowers and put them in a vase. You will need a packet of tissue paper, a pipe cleaner, a ruler and pencil, and a twig.

1. Lay eight layers of tissue paper in a pile. Mark a rectangle roughly 4.5 inches (11 cm) by 8 inches (20 cm). Then cut through all the paper layers, keeping them together in a pile.

2. Fold over one of the long edges about a half an inch (1 cm). Then fold it the other way and continue until all of the paper is folded like an accordian.

3. Tie a pipe cleaner tightly around the middle and wind the other end of the pipe cleaner around the twig. Gently open the tissue petals.

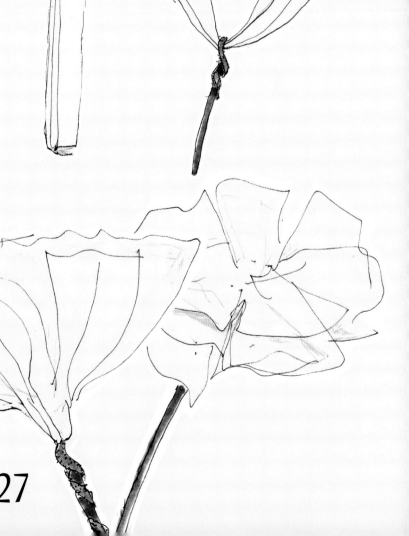

Be a spring scientist

Discover some spring science by changing the color of a flower and showing how plants help to make rain!

Color magic

When plants start to grow in the spring, they need water. You can prove this by turning a white flower a different color. You will need a white carnation, a jar of water, and some food coloring.

Drop food coloring into the water jar to make it dark. Then put the carnation stem into it.

Before long, your carnation will change color! That's because plants suck up water through their stems. Can you see where the dye has traveled through the petals?

Make stripes

To make a two-colored carnation, cut the stem in two about halfway up (as shown). Put one half in a jar of colored water and the other half in a jar of clear water. The next day, the flower will be half colored and half white.

The invisible plant secret

Did you know that plants help to make rain? Here's how to prove it. You'll need a small potted plant, a dish, a clear plastic bag, and some water.

1. Put the plant on the dish and water it. Set it on a sunny windowsill.

2. Gently put the plastic bag over the plant. Either tie the bag around the stem or tuck it under the pot.

Look at your experiment a day later. Has your plant made any rain?

After a while, the inside surface of the plastic bag will get wet. That's because plants send water vapor into the air through tiny leaf-holes called pores. This is called evaporation, and plants all over the world do it. The water vapor rises into the air and helps to make clouds and rain.

Words to remember

bulb A bud, some tiny leaves, and a store of food inside a round shape. A bulb can sprout and grow into a plant.

equator The imaginary line around the middle of Earth.

equinox A time of year when day and night are the same length. There are two equinoxes every year. One equinox signals the beginning of spring, and the other begins fall.

frogspawn Frog eggs inside balls of jelly. The eggs hatch into tadpoles.

hemispheres The northern and southern halves of Earth.

herbivore An animal that eats only plants. Cows, sheep, and goats are herbivores.

migration A journey some animals make between a summer home and a winter home.

nectar The sweet liquid inside a flower. Insects feed on nectar.

pollen Tiny grains inside a flower. A flower needs pollen grains from another similar flower before it can grow fruit and seeds.

rainbow A curve that appears in the sky when sunlight splits into different colors.

season A time of the year that has a particular kind of weather and temperature.

seed drill A machine farmers use to plant seeds in fields during the spring.

spectrum The different colors that make up sunlight. They are red, orange, yellow, green, blue, indigo, and violet.

tadpole A baby frog. Tadpoles hatch in the spring from frogspawn.

temperature How hot or cold something is.

Index